The Red Bird

by Jim Lobes

Illustrated by Nancy Harrison

Target Skill Review

PEARSON
Scott Foresman

Jim is in the red tent.

Mom said, "Jim, look at the red bird.
Can you spot it?"

3

 The red bird tugs at the soft mop.

The red bird tugs at six hats.

 The red bird tugs at a little twig.

What will the red bird do?

I can not spot it.

I can spot it.

The red bird will fix the best nest.